Needle Crafts 15

# PATCHWORK 2

SEARCH PRESS
Tunbridge Wells

## INTRODUCTION

Patchwork II describes ten different methods of patchwork, and follows on from the first patchwork book in this series (Needle Crafts 4) which covered the basic techniques. Machine Patchwork, with particular relation to quilts, is included in Needle Crafts 19.

## CONSTRUCTION

Small and intricate shapes are best put together by the paper and patch and oversewing method described in Needle Crafts 4, and shown here in Fig 1a.

A quicker method, especially for geometric and larger patches, is to sew the pieces together with a ¼"(6mm) seam. This is sometimes called Machine Patchwork, and is shown in Fig 1b.

A third method is to sew the pieces, by hand or by machine, on to a backing fabric, as in Fig 1c.

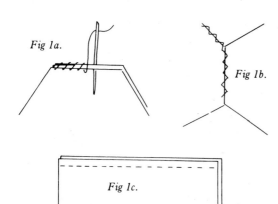

*Fig 1a.*

*Fig 1b.*

*Fig 1c.*

*Methods of joining patches*

## TEMPLATES

Commercial templates are available in all sizes and shapes. If you make your own, the method varies according to the particular patchwork technique in mind. Draw the required shape on squared paper using a ruler, as in Fig 2.

The paper and patch method does not need a seam allowance. Glue the squared paper to a piece of card and cut through both layers accurately along the drawn lines. Machine patchwork should have a ¼"(6mm) seam allowance all round. Add this to the squared paper shape before cutting out.

These templates can be used more than once, but if they are going to be used many times it is a good idea to make several of each shape.

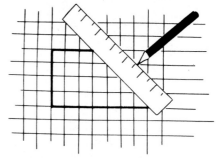

*Fig 2 Drawing template shapes on squared paper*

## DYEING

Fabrics for patchwork are often a motley collection. Fabrics in different colours can be unified by simple dyeing with a commercial dye. Collect together enough pieces of a suitable weight for one article, and put them all in a dyebath of a chosen colour. They will come out in all sorts of different shades and tones of that colour, and can be used together to make interesting colour schemes.

*Opposite page  2. Patterns which suggest three dimensions by the use of tone and shape.*

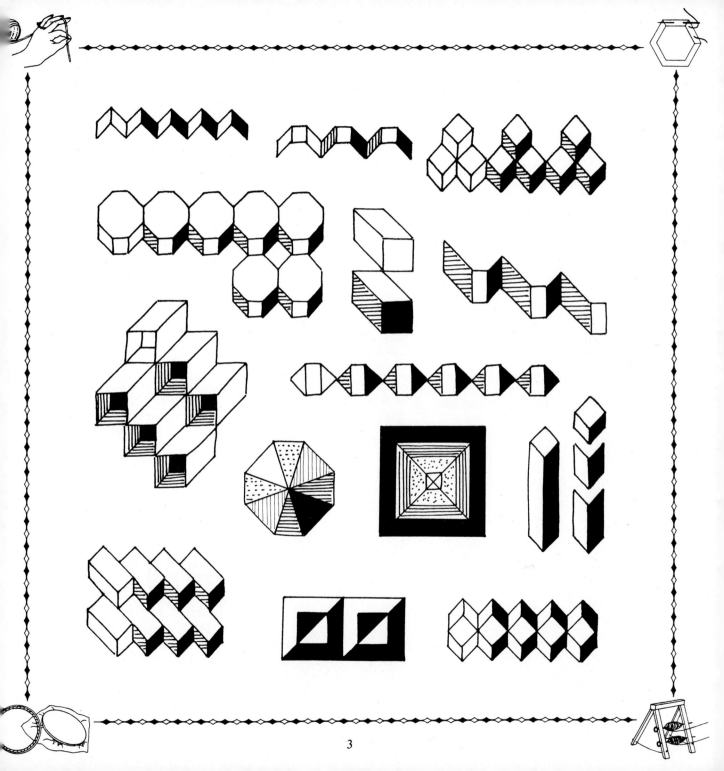

## METHOD VI.

### APPLIED PATCHWORK

Most types of patchwork can be made up, and then applied to a plain piece of fabric. This is quicker than making a whole patchwork article, and the plain areas show up the pattern. The applied patchwork can be placed centrally, arranged as separate motifs, or used as a border. Keep the overall shape simple and try to avoid awkward corners and sharp points, as these are difficult to deal with.

### Design ideas

Stars or rosettes made up of triangles, diamonds or hexagons can be applied to a square of fabric and used for a bag or cushion, to make the top of a box or as a centrepiece for a quilt. Patchwork borders can be applied all round.

Flowers or leaves can be built up from triangles and squares, and abstract patterns from a combination of diamonds, octagons and squares. Curved shapes are especially suitable for applied patchwork, as it is easier to apply than to piece them. Strips of patchwork can be applied across the yoke or around the sleeve of ready-made clothes to add colour and individuality.

### Preparation

Make up the patchwork and press it on the wrong side. If the paper and patch method is used the edges are already folded, but the papers should be taken

*page 4:*
**Ludo Board.** *Handstitched patchwork in cottons and polycottons with machine applied baskets and flowers. Mounted on to thin foam sheeting and backed with cotton. Single Suffolk Puffs are used for counters (**Sheila Bleasby**).*

*page 5:*
**Clamshell Patchwork Cushion.** *An overall pattern of Clamshell Patchwork. The two opposing rows of scales are joined with circular patches in the centre (**Pamela Watts**).*

out and the turnings pressed again to make them lie flat. Thicker fabrics and felt and leather can be left with a raw edge, but otherwise a ¼"(6mm) hem is turned under if required.

Lay the patchwork in position on the plain fabric, matching the grain if possible. Pin or tack all round the shape. Do this with the work lying flat to avoid puckers.

### Sewing

The patchwork can be applied by hand or by machine. Sew the folded edge to the plain fabric with hem stitch, slip stitch or stab stitch – slip stitch being the least visible. Alternatively a small running stitch can be worked close to the edge.

Raw edges can be covered with herringbone stitch, or swing-stitched by machine (Fig 3).

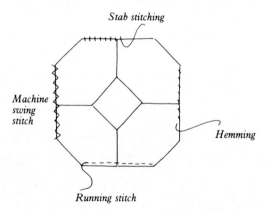

*Fig 3 Applying patchwork to a background fabric*

### Finishing

Press carefully on the right side over a thick towel.

*Opposite page 6. Motifs for Applied Patchwork.*

## METHOD VII.

### CRAZY AND RANDOM PATCHWORK

Crazy patchwork uses scraps of fabric of any shape or size, which are stitched to a backing fabric, usually cotton or calico. Traditionally feather stitching or herringbone covered the raw edges, and today machine zigzag or satin stitch can be used instead. The surface stitching should be worked in one-colour thread over the whole piece to unify it. Most types of fabric are suitable including silks, wools, velvet and leather – but it is best to keep to one type of fabric in one article.

Random patchwork consists of geometric shapes, usually squares and rectangles, of varying sizes, which are fitted together more or less haphazardly and sewn to a backing fabric in the same way as Crazy patchwork. Occasionally it may be pieced.

### Design ideas

As this form of patchwork is made from many different shapes and sizes the design possibilities are more limited than with other forms of patchwork. The size of the pieces can be graded from small to large in one article. The pieces can be put together to form squares or triangles or wide strips, which are then sewn together with a ¼″(6mm) seam to make a more controlled design.

### Traditional technique with plain backing
### Preparation

Cut the scraps to a convenient size and trim any frayed or curved edges. Cut a piece of cotton or calico

page 8:
**Child's Waistcoat**. *Random Patchwork in related colours, quilted by hand after assembly (**Valerie Harding**).*

page 9:
**Child's Anorak**. *Crazy Patchwork in cotton used on a commercial pattern. Embroidered in buttonhole twist (**Margaret Cheetham**).*

slightly larger than is needed, and mark the area to be covered with a hard pencil. Starting from one corner, lay the shapes on the calico overlapping the raw edges by about ¼″(6mm). Pin carefully.

### Sewing

Sew around the overlapping edges with running stitch. Add more pieces, pin and sew. Continue until the whole area is covered. Finally, work and embroidery stitch over the running stitches.

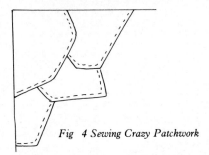

*Fig 4 Sewing Crazy Patchwork*

### Modern technique with padded backing

This makes a more solid fabric, and is stitched by machine. It can be done by hand but the results are not so satisfactory.

### Preparation

Cut the fabric pieces together with thin wadding, and treat as one. Pin the pieces to the backing, touching each other.

### Sewing

Work close machine zigzag all round the edge of each padded piece. Place a few more pieces-plus-wadding next to the stitched ones, pin and sew. Continue until the whole area is covered.

### Finishing

The first method is lined when the article is made up. The second method quilts the patchwork and does not need lining.

## METHOD VIII.

### CLAMSHELL PATCHWORK.

This method is also known as 'Shell' or 'Fish-scale' patchwork from the shape of the templates. These templates are made in pairs, one solid metal and one slightly larger transparent window template. It is better to buy these than to make them, since constructing them accurately is difficult. The paper and patch method is used to construct the shapes, which are built up in overlapping rows to form a fabric, each row being stitched to the previous one. Choose soft but firmly woven fabrics, and use matching thread.

### Design ideas

As Clamshell patchwork generally produces an overall design of the same shapes, variety is best achieved by changes of colour, pattern and texture. The curved lines and unified pattern are ideal for small items, and small areas make a good applied decoration for clothes and household linen. Pin out the patches on insulation board to plan a design.

### Preparation

Prepare a paper patch as follows: place the solid template on thin card, draw round with a sharp pencil, and cut on this line. Prepare a number of fabric patches as follows: place the window template on the straight grain of the fabric, hold the two together or draw round with a soft pencil, and cut round the shape.

### Sewing

Pin the paper shape in the centre of the *right side* of a fabric patch as in Fig 5a. Turn them over, and with the wrong side of the fabric uppermost tack down the semi-circular edge, making small pleated folds, and following exactly the curve of the paper, as in Fig 5b. Make sure the fabric is not sewn to the paper pattern. Unpin the paper and use it for the next patch. Use a new paper shape when the old one becomes worn. Make the required number of patches.

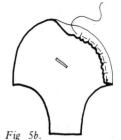

*Fig 5a. Pinning paper to fabric.*  *Fig 5b. Turning under a hem.*

To assemble the patches, pin the first row on a board in a straight line, right side up, with the sides of each patch just touching. Pin the second row in place, overlapping the first by ¼"(6mm) and covering the raw edges. Hem each row to the next along the convex edge.

Circular patches can be made to join two areas of scales placed in opposite directions, as in the cushion on page 5. If the patchwork is to be applied, the hemming is taken through all layers of fabric.

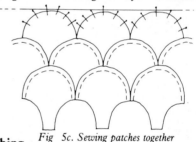

*Fig 5c. Sewing patches together*

### Finishing

Clamshell patchwork should be lined. The raw edges of the last row can be concealed in a seam where applicable or covered with a strip of fabric.

*page 12:*
**Table Mat and Napkin**. *Applied Clamshell Patchwork* (**Pamela Watts**).

*page 13:*
**Jacket**. *Cathedral Window Patchwork. A calico background with velvet central squares in four shades of brown at the borders. The remaining central squares are in calico, and all patches are stab stitched in place* (**Christine Cooper**).

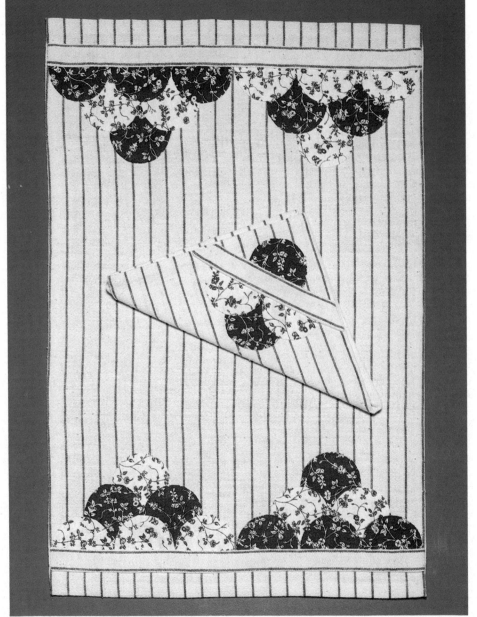

## METHOD IX.

## CATHEDRAL WINDOW PATCHWORK.

Cathedral window patchwork differs from most other kinds in that it is three-dimensional and more solid in construction. It is generally made from doubled calico squares, pairs of which are joined with a seam which is covered with a small square of coloured cotton laid diagonally down the seam. Other fabrics such as satin, silk or patterned cotton can be used. The small squares can be of different fabrics and textures. This patchwork can be sewn by hand or by machine.

### Design ideas

The plain calico background has a unifying effect, so that small treasured scraps can be used for the coloured squares. The latter could also be embroidered with a single motif, or consist of pieces of canvas work, or fabric that has been stitched, dyed or painted.

The small squares of colour can be arranged in patterns such as diamonds or diagonal strips, or shaded from light to dark as in the jacket on page 00. It is possible to use a single layer of leather instead of the doubled calico, turning the folds to show the suede on the reverse.

A row of tiny 'windows' can be used as a belt, a single one as a pocket, or two together as a pincushion, as on back cover.

### By Hand

### Preparation

Cut a square of calico about four times as large as is required for the finished square – for example, cut a 8¼″(21cm) square for a 4″(10cm) finished size. The sides should be on the straight grain of the fabric. Turn in a ¼″(6mm) hem all round the edge (Fig 6a).

Fold each corner to the centre and pin (Fig 6b). Again fold the corners to the centre and pin. Stitch

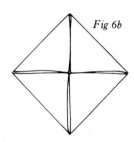

Fig 6a

Fig 6b

all four corners together firmly, sewing through to the back.

Make a number of squares.

### Sewing

Place two squares face to face with the folded edges level with each other, and oversew them together along one edge (Fig 6c). Open them flat, and place on a table smooth side down.

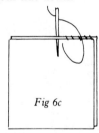

Fig 6c

Cut a 1¾″(4.3cm) square of coloured cotton and place it diagonally over the join. Roll the folds of the calico back over the raw edges and hem them, or secure them with running stitch (Fig 6d). This stitching should go right through to the back to hold all the layers together. Make rows of finished windows

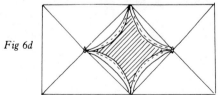

Fig 6d

and then sew the rows together to make the article, adding more coloured squares between the rows.

## By Machine

Before attempting this method, make a square by the hand method so that the process is thoroughly understood. In the end, method 2 is quicker and easier, but it needs practice. Cut three card templates with the following measurements:

(a) 9″ (22.7cm) square.
(b) 4″ x 8″ (5cm × 10cm).
(c) 2¼″ (5.7cm) square.

Lay template (a) on the calico with the sides matching the grain, and draw round with a hard pencil. Cut along the drawn line. Fold the piece in half.

Place template (b) next to the fold and draw along the short edges only. Pin the layers together and seam along the short sides only. Trim the corners and press the seams open (Fig 7a).

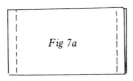

*Fig 7a*

Bring the seams together with the right sides facing and pin along the raw edges. Stitch, leaving an opening for turning (Fig 7b). Clip the corners and press the seams open. Turn the square right side out, press flat, and slip stitch the opening.

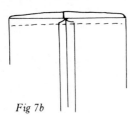

*Fig 7b*

Bring corners A and B together and make a sharp fold (X) at the centre of each side (Fig 7c). Draw lines from X to X on the seamed side of the square.

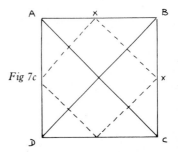

*Fig 7c*

This is the seam line for joining the squares. Match the drawn lines on two squares and stitch. Join a number of squares together in a row. Pin the four corners to the centre point of each square and stitch firmly together through all the layers.

Lay template (c) on the wrong side of the coloured cotton, draw round and cut out. Place it diagonally over the exposed seam between two calico squares and pin through all the layers. Turn the edges back over the coloured area and hem, stitching through all the layers.

## Finishing

No quilting, lining or edging is required, as this patchwork has no raw edges and is never less than two layers thick.

page 16:
**Cot Quilt**. *An example of a simple repeating pattern made interesting by subtle variations in colour, achieved by home dyeing (**Valerie Harding**).*

page 17:
**Snakes and Ladders Board**. *Handstitched patchwork in cottons. Spot quilted at each corner of the squares through thin foam sheeting. Embroidered felt snakes and macrame ladders (**Sheila Bleasby**).*

FIN

START

## METHOD X.

### BORDERS

Many kinds of patchwork make interesting borders which can be pieced or applied to the main fabric. The diagrams on the page opposite show how they can be built up from simple shapes.

A patchwork border will extend the area round a square of printed fabric or a piece of embroidery, and will also form a decorative frame. Borders can be placed on the edges of curtains, blinds or tablecloths, around the bottom of jackets or skirts, along yokes, and round cuffs and down the front of tops and dresses.

Most quilts, whatever the pattern, look better with a border. Medallion quilts are almost all border, with a small central area which is often of printed fabric. Some furnishing fabrics with a large motif would make an ideal centrepiece, surrounded with successive borders.

It is often a good idea to combine the same pattern on a different scale in one piece of work; for example to make a border of 2″(5cm) diamonds, then one of squares, then one of 4″(10cm) diamonds, and join them all together. The smaller shapes should be placed towards the middle of the article.

Corners can be a problem with borders, and several solutions are shown in the diagrams. If you are not sure how well a pattern will turn a corner, hold a small flat mirror at right angles to the pattern and adjust it until you see the result you want. If turning is too difficult, fill in the corner with a plain or pieced square.

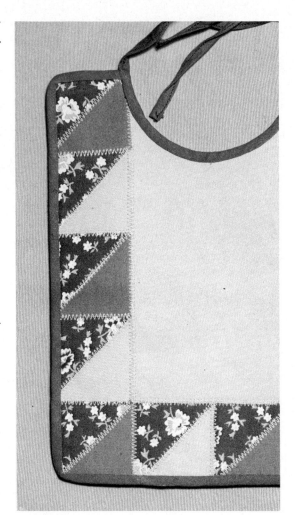

*page 21:*
**Bib** *with patchwork border, backed with towelling (***Valerie Harding***).*
**Tea Cosy** *An example of Seminole patchwork, which has been quilted (***Val Harding***).*
**Pin Cushion.** *An example of Cathedral window patchwork made by the machine method (***Lois Hennequin***).*

*Detail from page 21:*
*Bib with patchwork border, backed with towelling (***Valerie Harding***).*

*Opposite page 18. Borders, using squares, triangles, diamonds and half hexagons, plus strips of fabric.*

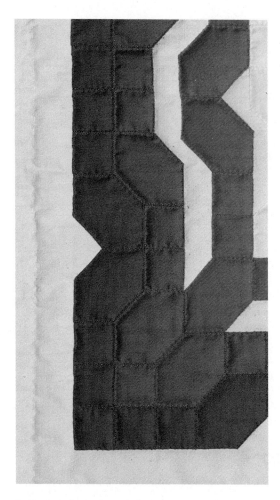
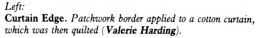

*Left:*
**Curtain Edge.** *Patchwork border applied to a cotton curtain, which was then quilted (***Valerie Harding***).*

*Right*
**Puff Patchwork Cot Quilt.** *Corner of cot quilt in Puff Patchwork in two colours (***Valerie Harding***).*

*A detail of strip patchwork from the back cover.*

## METHOD XI.

### STRIP PATCHWORK

Using strips of fabric in patchwork is an economical method which also makes for interesting patterns. A ruler or yardstick is a useful template and is always accurate.

### Design ideas

Long strips of fabric can be sewn together, then cut up across the seams and joined to other shapes, or to each other with the strips going in different directions.

Geometric shapes such as triangles can be sewn together in long strips, and then joined to plain fabric or to strips of other shapes.

Strips can be used to frame a central geometric shape, and can become wider at the outer edge. This looks particularly effective on cushions.

### Preparation

Lay the ruler on the back of the fabric along the grain and draw along the edge with a hard pencil or dressmaker's pencil. Include a ¼"(6mm) seam allowance in the width of the strip. Draw a number of strips of different widths and cut them out accurately. Lay two together and pin at intervals along one edge.

### Sewing

The best method is to machine stitch ¼"(6mm) from one edge, using the edge of the presser foot as a guide.

Press the seam to one side. Join all your strips together in pairs, and then join the pairs together.

### Finishing

This patchwork must be lined or backed, so that the edges do not fray.

*Opposite page 22. Patterns using strips of fabric, ribbon, or patchwork patterns such as triangles or squares, sewn together in various combinations.*

## METHOD XII.

### SEMINOLE PATCHWORK

This patchwork is an extension of strip piecing developed by the Seminole Indians of Florida. Fabric strips of varying widths are machined together, then cut into sections and resewn to make strips of patterns. The Seminoles used this technique to insert strips of brilliant colour into the plain fabric of shirts, skirts and dresses. Their method has now been adapted for use in quilts and other articles, using silks and patterned fabrics as well as thin cottons.

### Design ideas

For dress the Seminole patchwork is usually on a small scale with the strips varying in width from ¾″(1.5cm) to 1½″(3.7cm), including a ¼″(6mm) seam.

Furnishings and quilts use Seminole patchwork on a larger scale, the strips being 3″(7.5cm) wide or more.

The rows of joined strips can be cut and rearranged to produce an endless variety of patterns. Some of these are illustrated in the accompanying diagrams.

### Preparation

Cut the strips on the straight grain of the fabric, allowing ¼″(6mm) each side for seams. Make the strips longer than you think you will need as there is a certain amount of wastage when re-cutting them. Pin the strips together at intervals along one edge, right sides together.

*page 24:*
**Table mat**. *Patches applied to a vilene backing and zigzagged in place. The mat is backed with towelling (**Valerie Harding**).*

*page 25:*
**Seminole Yoke and Cuffs**. *A wild silk dress decorated with Seminole Indian Patchwork on cuffs and yoke in Thai silks. The shot fabrics give subtle contrast of tone instead of the traditional bold colour contrasts (**Val Tulloch**).*

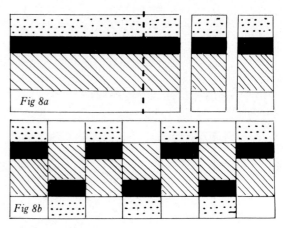

*Fig 8a*

*Fig 8b*

### Sewing

Stitch along the seam line and press the seam to one side.

When three or four strips have been sewn together, cut across them according to the diagrams and re-sew, again with a ¼″(6mm) seam. Two or more different patterned strips can be used in the same piece of work, separated by one or more strips of plain fabric.

### Finishing

The finished patchwork should be lined.

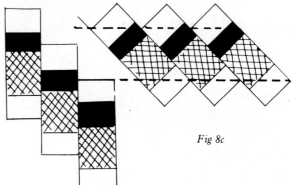

*Fig 8c*

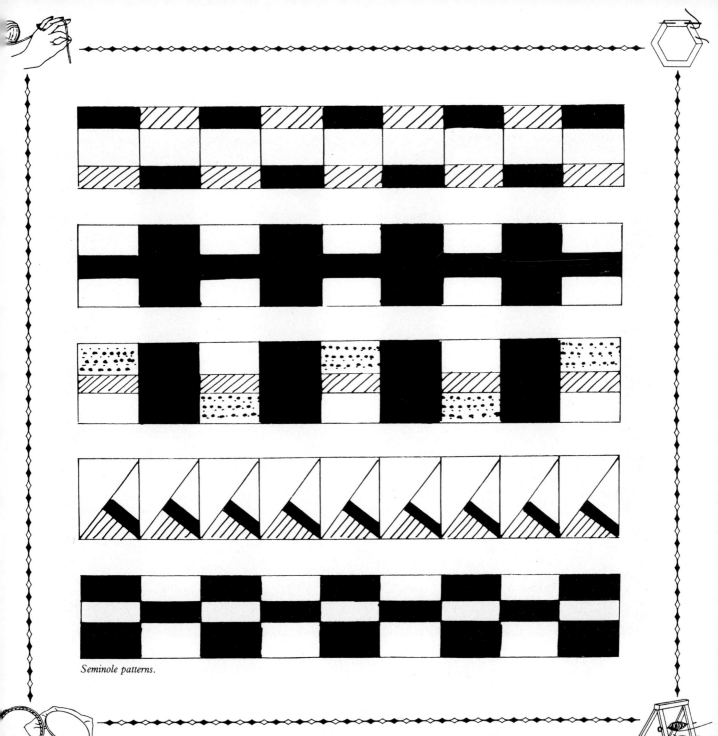

*Seminole patterns.*

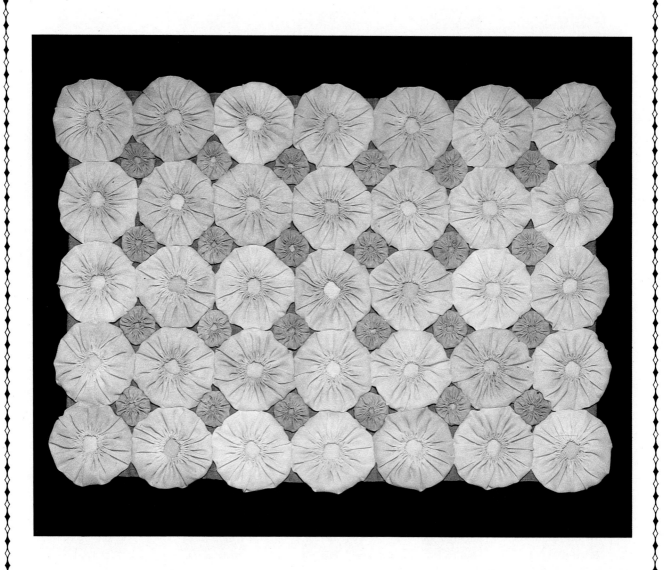

## METHOD XIII.

### SUFFOLK PUFFS

These are gathered circular patches which are sewn together with spaces left between them. Fine fabrics should be used, such as silk, organdie and soft cottons. These make up into a delicate openwork fabric which is valued for decorative effect and textural qualities. The gathered side of the circles is the right side. In any one article the fabric should be of the same weight and type.

### Design ideas

The design possibilities of Suffolk Puffs are based on variations of colour and scale. Strips of puffs in different sizes or colours can be sewn together to make patterns such as diagonals, chevrons or squares. Tiny puffs can be used as decorative ends to ribbons. Areas of puffs will add texture to fashion designs, such as sleeves on a wedding dress, but these should be in manmade fabrics as they cannot be ironed.

Small puffs can be placed inside large ones to add body and texture. It is also possible to pad or stuff the circles.

Toys can be made by threading puffs on to elastic or crochet cotton to make snakes, animals or dolls.

### Preparation

Lay a small plate or saucer on the back of the chosen fabric, draw round and cut out. The circle should be just over twice the size of the finished puff.

*page 28:*
**Suffolk Puff Pram Cover.** *Circles of cotton polyester voile sprayed with fabric paint using an air brush. Each puff has a small circle of quilting wadding, covered with a piece of voile, stitched in place in the centre before the edges were gathered. The cover is backed with voile (****Pamela Watts****).*

*page 29:*
**Flower pincushion**. *Raised Patchwork (****Valerie Harding****).*

### Sewing

Turn under a narrow hem on the wrong side and sew all round the circle with small running stitches (Fig 9a). Draw the thread up tightly and finish off by oversewing two or three times in one place (Fig 9b). Make a number of puffs.

Join the patches together from the back (the smooth side) with a few stitches at four separate points around the edge. This turns the circle into a shape which is nearly square (Fig 9c).

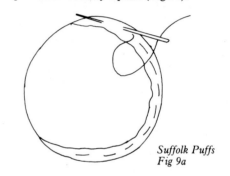

*Suffolk Puffs*
*Fig 9a*

*Fig 9b*

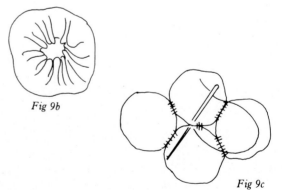

*Fig 9c*

### Finishing

The work may be left as it is, or backed with a fabric of a different colour which shows through the spaces.

## METHOD XIV.

### PUFF PATCHWORK

Puff patchwork is basically square or rectangular bags of fabric stuffed with wadding or scraps and sewn together. The back is flat and the front very raised.

It is a quick method of making a warm quilt, but can also be used for cushions or bags. Cotton fabric is best.

### Design ideas

The squares or rectangles can be of different sizes, as long as they all fit together without gaps. Rectangles can be arranged to make chevron patterns as in parquet flooring. If the squares are all the same size, colour can be used to make a pattern such as checkerboard or stripes or Greek crosses.

If transparent fabric is used for the top layer, the filling can be coloured to make a delicate colour scheme suitable, for example, for a pram cover.

### Preparation

Cut one 2"(5cm) square and one 2½"(7.5cm) square of fabric. Place the wrong sides together and pin at the corners.

Pleat the excess fabric at the centres of the sides and pin the layers together. Prepare a number of these.

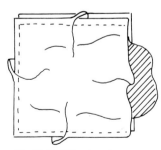

*Fig 10 Puff Patchwork*

### Sewing

Stitch around three sides of each square, preferably by machine, leaving a ½"(6mm) seam. Insert wadding, scraps or a nylon stocking through the opening, being careful not to stuff too tightly (Fig 10). Make a pleat on the fourth side and stitch it closed. When a number of puffs have been made, place them face to face and stitch them together over the previous seam.

### Finishing

Press the seams open. Back the puffs with a piece of plain fabric and bind the edges with narrow strips of fabric.

## METHOD XV.

### RAISED PATCHWORK

Raised patchwork is made by stuffing double-sided shapes with wadding. These are then joined to make flat articles such as quilts, or more firmly stuffed for three-dimensional shapes.

### Design ideas

All kinds of geometric shapes may be used, as well as free shapes such as flower petals. Stuffed shapes can be built up into three-dimensional pieces such as pincushions, flowers, Christmas tree ornaments and toys.

### Preparation

Make a card template of the shape required, including a ¼"(6mm) seam allowance. Lay this template on the wrong side of the fabric, and draw round the shape. Draw two pieces for every finished patch. Cut round the shapes.

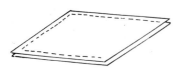

*Fig 11 Raised Patchwork*

## Sewing

Place two pieces face to face and seam around leaving a small opening. Turn inside out. Stuff lightly with wadding. Slip stitch the opening together (Fig 11).

When a number of patches have been made they can be joined by oversewing or fagotting.

*Front cover:*
**Suffolk Puff Pram Cover** *See page 30.*

*Back cover:*
**Bag**. *Strip patchwork, quilted by machine (* **Valerie Harding** *).*

*Inside front cover:*
**Cushion**. *The patches have been applied to a vilene background with machine zigzag. The pattern gives a three-dimensional effect (* **Valerie Harding** *).*

**Acknowledgments**
Series editor: Kit Pyman

Text by Valerie Harding. Drawings by Valerie Harding. Clamshell section by Pamela Watt. Photographs by Search Press Studios.

Text, illustrations, arrangement and typography copyright © Search Press Limited 1983.

First published in Great Britain in 1983 by Search Press Limited, Wellwood, North Farm Road, Tunbridge Wells, Kent TN2 3DR.

Reprinted 1984, 1985, 1986, 1988, 1989

ISBN 0 85532 450 3

Made and printed in Spain by A. G. Elkar, S. Coop. Autonomía, 71 - 48012-Bilbao - Spain